Garden of

GRATITUDE

A 52-WEEK GRATITUDE JOURNAL

GOOD VIBES PUBLISHING CO.

THIS BOOK BELONGS TO:

Why Gratitude?

A simple daily gratitude practice may not seem like much, but the benefits are profound.

- **Gratitude can make us happier.** Practicing gratitude reduces toxic emotions like envy and regret.
- **Gratitude can reduce stress and therefore improve health.**
- **Gratitude can increase good energy.** There's a Tony Robbins saying, "Where attention goes, energy flows."
- **Gratitude can improve sleep quality.** When we focus on the good things, there are less bad things to keep us up at night.
- **Gratitude can increase resilience.** We all face challenges.
- **Gratitude can improve our relationships.**
- **Gratitude can increase our empathy.** By being grateful for what we do have, we have more empathy and compassion for the struggles of others.

Daily Affirmations

CHOOSE AFFIRMATIONS THAT SPEAK TO YOU AND WHAT YOU NEED EACH WEEK.

I am somebody and my life has purpose.
I am beautiful just as I am.
I am strong and can get through anything.
I have a 100% success rate of getting through hard days.
I can do hard things.
I am doing my best and it is enough.
I deserve to be happy.
I am worthy of love.
I love myself for exactly who I am.
I am the perfect age today.
I have power over my mood and can choose how I feel.
I am at peace with my body.
I do not let others hold me back from my goals.
I treat myself with love and respect.
I am patient with myself, even when I make mistakes.
I am grateful for this day and will make the most of it.
I am getting better every day.
I am complete just as I am.
I am exactly where I need to be.
No one else gets to define me. I decide for myself.
I can reach any goal I set my mind to.
My past does not define who I am today.
I trust my wisdom and intuition. I know what is best for me.
I do not need to impress anyone.
I accept who I am, even if it makes others uncomfortable.
I am successful, confident, attractive and happy.

"

THE SECRET OF CHANGE
IS TO FOCUS ALL OF YOUR

energy

NOT ON FIGHTING THE OLD,
BUT ON BUILDING THE NEW.

"

Socrates

Set Your Intentions:

Gratitude is something that we can practice and a skill that can be improved over time. Some days expressing gratitude will be easier than others.

Start by sharing your intentions for starting a gratitude practice here, so you can come back to read this on days when you are struggling.

Why do you want to start expressing your gratitude? What are you hoping to achieve from this practice?

A Garden of Gratitude

> "GRATITUDE IS A POWERFUL CATALYST FOR HAPPINESS. IT'S THE SPARK THAT LIGHTS A FIRE OF JOY IN YOUR SOUL."
> – AMY COLLETTE

Today I am grateful for...   Date

1._____
2._____
3._____
4._____

Today I am grateful for...   Date

1._____
2._____
3._____
4._____

Today I am grateful for...   Date

1._____
2._____
3._____
4._____

Today I am grateful for...   Date

1._____
2._____
3._____
4._____

Today I am grateful for...   Date

1._____
2._____
3._____
4._____

Today I am grateful for...   Date

1._____
2._____
3._____
4._____

Today I am grateful for...   Date

1._____
2._____
3._____
4._____

My Affirmations for Next Week:

A Garden of Gratitude

BE THANKFUL FOR WHAT YOU HAVE; YOU'LL END UP HAVING MORE. IF YOU CONCENTRATE ON WHAT YOU DON'T HAVE, YOU WILL NEVER, EVER HAVE ENOUGH."   – OPRAH WINFREY

Today I am grateful for...   Date

1._____
2._____
3._____
4._____

Today I am grateful for...   Date

1._____
2._____
3._____
4._____

Today I am grateful for...   Date

1._____
2._____
3._____
4._____

Today I am grateful for...   Date

1._____
2._____
3._____
4._____

Today I am grateful for...   Date

1._____
2._____
3._____
4._____

Today I am grateful for...   Date

1._____
2._____
3._____
4._____

Today I am grateful for...   Date

1._____
2._____
3._____
4._____

My Affirmations for Next Week:

A Garden of Gratitude

> "GRATITUDE FOR THE PRESENT MOMENT AND THE FULLNESS OF LIFE NOW IS THE TRUE PROSPERITY." – ECKHART TOLLE

Today I am grateful for...   Date

1._____
2._____
3._____
4._____

Today I am grateful for...   Date

1._____
2._____
3._____
4._____

Today I am grateful for...   Date

1._____
2._____
3._____
4._____

Today I am grateful for...   Date

1._____
2._____
3._____
4._____

Today I am grateful for...   Date

1._____
2._____
3._____
4._____

Today I am grateful for...   Date

1._____
2._____
3._____
4._____

Today I am grateful for...   Date

1._____
2._____
3._____
4._____

My Affirmations for Next Week:

A Garden of Gratitude

> "GRATITUDE MAKES SENSE OF OUR PAST,
> BRINGS PEACE FOR TODAY,
> AND CREATES A VISION FOR TOMORROW."
> – MELODY BEATTIE

Today I am grateful for...   Date

1._____
2._____
3._____
4._____

Today I am grateful for...   Date

1._____
2._____
3._____
4._____

Today I am grateful for...   Date

1._____
2._____
3._____
4._____

Today I am grateful for...   Date

1._____
2._____
3._____
4._____

Today I am grateful for...   Date

1._____
2._____
3._____
4._____

Today I am grateful for...   Date

1._____
2._____
3._____
4._____

Today I am grateful for...   Date

1._____
2._____
3._____
4._____

My Affirmations for Next Week:

A Garden of Gratitude

> "GRATITUDE AND ATTITUDE
> ARE NOT CHALLENGES;
> THEY ARE CHOICES."
> – ROBERT BRAATHE

Today I am grateful for...   Date

1._____
2._____
3._____
4._____

Today I am grateful for...   Date

1._____
2._____
3._____
4._____

Today I am grateful for...   Date

1._____
2._____
3._____
4._____

Today I am grateful for...   Date

1._____
2._____
3._____
4._____

Today I am grateful for...   Date

1._____
2._____
3._____
4._____

Today I am grateful for...   Date

1._____
2._____
3._____
4._____

Today I am grateful for...   Date

1._____
2._____
3._____
4._____

My Affirmations for Next Week:

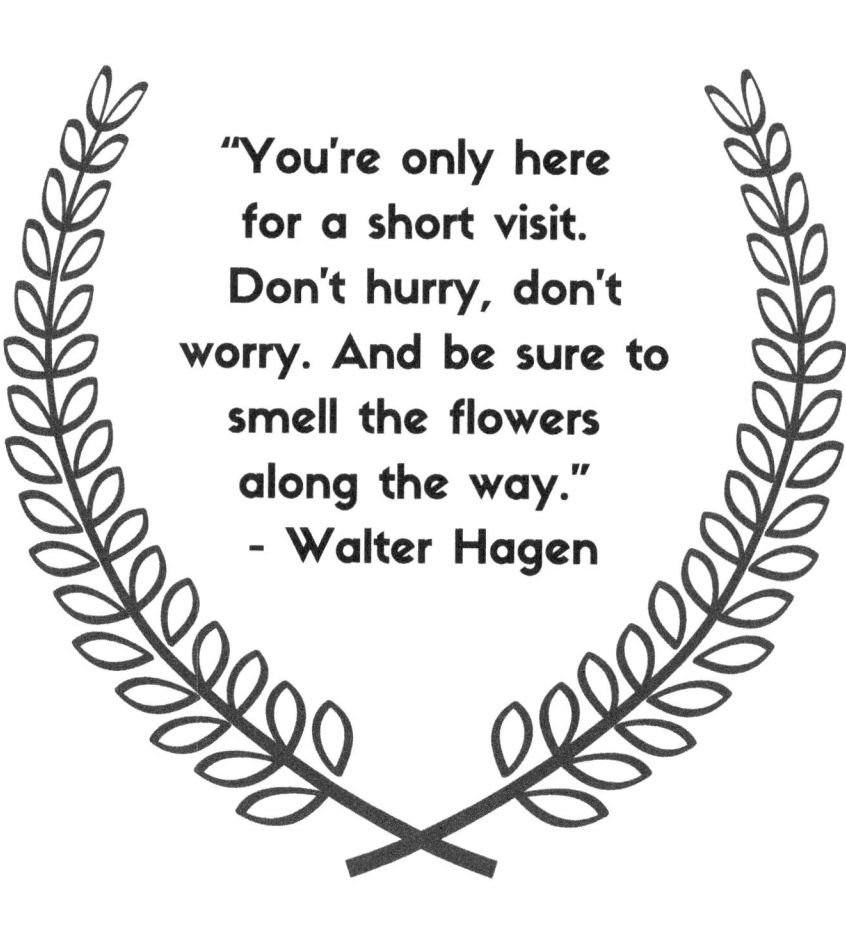

"You're only here for a short visit. Don't hurry, don't worry. And be sure to smell the flowers along the way."
- Walter Hagen

Reflection:

What are some things in life that disrupt your feelings of gratitude the most? List the things that really bother you! How can a shift in perspective help you choose happiness more often?

A Garden of Gratitude

> "WEAR GRATITUDE LIKE A CLOAK,
> AND IT WILL FEED
> EVERY CORNER OF YOUR LIFE."
> – RUMI

Today I am grateful for...   Date

1._____
2._____
3._____
4._____

Today I am grateful for...   Date

1._____
2._____
3._____
4._____

Today I am grateful for...   Date

1._____
2._____
3._____
4._____

Today I am grateful for...   Date

1._____
2._____
3._____
4._____

Today I am grateful for...   Date

1._____
2._____
3._____
4._____

Today I am grateful for...   Date

1._____
2._____
3._____
4._____

Today I am grateful for...   Date

1._____
2._____
3._____
4._____

My Affirmations for Next Week:

A Garden of Gratitude

> "WHAT SEPARATES PRIVILEGE
> FROM ENTITLEMENT - IS GRATITUDE."
> – BRENE BROWN

Today I am grateful for...   Date

1._____
2._____
3._____
4._____

Today I am grateful for...   Date

1._____
2._____
3._____
4._____

Today I am grateful for...   Date

1._____
2._____
3._____
4._____

Today I am grateful for...   Date

1._____
2._____
3._____
4._____

Today I am grateful for...   Date

1._____
2._____
3._____
4._____

Today I am grateful for...   Date

1._____
2._____
3._____
4._____

Today I am grateful for...   Date

1._____
2._____
3._____
4._____

My Affirmations for Next Week:

A Garden of Gratitude

"IN ORDINARY LIFE, WE HARDLY REALIZE THAT WE RECEIVE A GREAT DEAL MORE THAN WE GIVE, AND THAT IT IS ONLY WITH GRATITUDE THAT LIFE BECOMES RICH." – DIETRICH BONHOEFFER

Today I am grateful for...   Date

1._____
2._____
3._____
4._____

Today I am grateful for...   Date

1._____
2._____
3._____
4._____

Today I am grateful for...   Date

1._____
2._____
3._____
4._____

Today I am grateful for...   Date

1._____
2._____
3._____
4._____

Today I am grateful for...   Date

1._____
2._____
3._____
4._____

Today I am grateful for...   Date

1._____
2._____
3._____
4._____

Today I am grateful for...   Date

1._____
2._____
3._____
4._____

My Affirmations for Next Week:

A Garden of Gratitude

> "GRATITUDE IS NOT ONLY THE GREATEST OF VIRTUES
> BUT THE PARENT OF ALL OTHERS."
> – MARCUS TULLIUS CICERO

Today I am grateful for...   Date

1._____
2._____
3._____
4._____

Today I am grateful for...   Date

1._____
2._____
3._____
4._____

Today I am grateful for...   Date

1._____
2._____
3._____
4._____

Today I am grateful for...　　　　　Date

1._____
2._____
3._____
4._____

Today I am grateful for...　　　　　Date

1._____
2._____
3._____
4._____

Today I am grateful for...　　　　　Date

1._____
2._____
3._____
4._____

Today I am grateful for...　　　　　Date

1._____
2._____
3._____
4._____

My Affirmations for Next Week:

A Garden of Gratitude

> "GRATITUDE WILL SHIFT YOU
> TO A HIGHER FREQUENCY,
> AND YOU WILL ATTRACT MUCH BETTER THINGS."
> – RHONDA BYRNE

Today I am grateful for...   Date

1._____
2._____
3._____
4._____

Today I am grateful for...   Date

1._____
2._____
3._____
4._____

Today I am grateful for...   Date

1._____
2._____
3._____
4._____

Today I am grateful for...   Date

1._____
2._____
3._____
4._____

Today I am grateful for...   Date

1._____
2._____
3._____
4._____

Today I am grateful for...   Date

1._____
2._____
3._____
4._____

Today I am grateful for...   Date

1._____
2._____
3._____
4._____

My Affirmations for Next Week:

"Change your thoughts and you change your world."

– NORMAN VINCENT PEALE

Dig Deep:

What are some of the negative thoughts that destroy your peace? How can you change these thought patterns so that you can live a more peaceful life?

_____

_____

_____

_____

_____

_____

_____

_____

_____

_____

_____

_____

_____

_____

_____

_____

_____

_____

_____

A Garden of Gratitude

> "GRATITUDE HELPS YOU TO GROW AND EXPAND;
> GRATITUDE BRINGS JOY AND LAUGHTER INTO YOUR
> LIFE AND INTO THE LIVES OF ALL THOSE AROUND YOU."
> – EILEEN CADDY

Today I am grateful for...   Date

1._____
2._____
3._____
4._____

Today I am grateful for...   Date

1._____
2._____
3._____
4._____

Today I am grateful for...   Date

1._____
2._____
3._____
4._____

Today I am grateful for...   Date

1._____
2._____
3._____
4._____

Today I am grateful for...   Date

1._____
2._____
3._____
4._____

Today I am grateful for...   Date

1._____
2._____
3._____
4._____

Today I am grateful for...   Date

1._____
2._____
3._____
4._____

My Affirmations for Next Week:

A Garden of Gratitude

"GRATITUDE LOOKS TO THE PAST
AND LOVE TO THE PRESENT;
FEAR, AVARICE, LUST, AND AMBITION LOOK AHEAD."
— C.S. LEWIS

Today I am grateful for...   Date

1._____
2._____
3._____
4._____

Today I am grateful for...   Date

1._____
2._____
3._____
4._____

Today I am grateful for...   Date

1._____
2._____
3._____
4._____

Today I am grateful for...   Date

1._____
2._____
3._____
4._____

Today I am grateful for...   Date

1._____
2._____
3._____
4._____

Today I am grateful for...   Date

1._____
2._____
3._____
4._____

Today I am grateful for...   Date

1._____
2._____
3._____
4._____

My Affirmations for Next Week:

A Garden of Gratitude

> "ENJOY THE LITTLE THINGS,
> FOR ONE DAY YOU MAY LOOK BACK
> AND REALIZE THEY WERE THE BIG THINGS."
> -ROBERT BRAULT

Today I am grateful for...   Date

1._____
2._____
3._____
4._____

Today I am grateful for...   Date

1._____
2._____
3._____
4._____

Today I am grateful for...   Date

1._____
2._____
3._____
4._____

Today I am grateful for...   Date

1._____
2._____
3._____
4._____

Today I am grateful for...   Date

1._____
2._____
3._____
4._____

Today I am grateful for...   Date

1._____
2._____
3._____
4._____

Today I am grateful for...   Date

1._____
2._____
3._____
4._____

My Affirmations for Next Week:

A Garden of Gratitude

> "THE MORE GRATEFUL I AM,
> THE MORE BEAUTY I SEE."
> – MARY DAVIS

Today I am grateful for...   Date

1._____
2._____
3._____
4._____

Today I am grateful for...   Date

1._____
2._____
3._____
4._____

Today I am grateful for...   Date

1._____
2._____
3._____
4._____

Today I am grateful for...   Date

1._____
2._____
3._____
4._____

Today I am grateful for...   Date

1._____
2._____
3._____
4._____

Today I am grateful for...   Date

1._____
2._____
3._____
4._____

Today I am grateful for...   Date

1._____
2._____
3._____
4._____

My Affirmations for Next Week:

A Garden of Gratitude

> "PIGLET NOTICED THAT EVEN THOUGH
> HE HAD A VERY SMALL HEART,
> IT COULD HOLD A RATHER LARGE AMOUNT OF
> GRATITUDE." – A.A. MILNE

Today I am grateful for...   Date

1._____
2._____
3._____
4._____

Today I am grateful for...   Date

1._____
2._____
3._____
4._____

Today I am grateful for...   Date

1._____
2._____
3._____
4._____

Today I am grateful for...   Date

1._____
2._____
3._____
4._____

Today I am grateful for...   Date

1._____
2._____
3._____
4._____

Today I am grateful for...   Date

1._____
2._____
3._____
4._____

Today I am grateful for...   Date

1._____
2._____
3._____
4._____

My Affirmations for Next Week:

"With the new day comes new strength and new thoughts."

– ELEANOR ROOSEVELT

A New Day:

Buddha once said, "Each morning we are born again. What we do today is what matters most."

How can you start each day in such a way that you are able to start fresh, stay focused and choose happy?

_____

_____

_____

_____

_____

_____

_____

_____

_____

_____

_____

_____

_____

_____

A Garden of Gratitude

> "THE ROOT OF JOY
> IS GRATEFULNESS."
> - DAVID STEINDL-RAST

Today I am grateful for...   Date

1._____
2._____
3._____
4._____

Today I am grateful for...   Date

1._____
2._____
3._____
4._____

Today I am grateful for...   Date

1._____
2._____
3._____
4._____

Today I am grateful for...   Date

1._____
2._____
3._____
4._____

Today I am grateful for...   Date

1._____
2._____
3._____
4._____

Today I am grateful for...   Date

1._____
2._____
3._____
4._____

Today I am grateful for...   Date

1._____
2._____
3._____
4._____

My Affirmations for Next Week:

A Garden of Gratitude

"GRATITUDE UNLOCKS THE FULLNESS OF LIFE. IT TURNS WHAT WE HAVE INTO ENOUGH, AND MORE. IT TURNS DENIAL INTO ACCEPTANCE, CHAOS TO ORDER, CONFUSION TO CLARITY. IT CAN TURN A MEAL INTO A FEAST, A HOUSE INTO A HOME, AND A STRANGER INTO A FRIEND." — MELODY BEATTIE

Today I am grateful for...   Date

1._____
2._____
3._____
4._____

Today I am grateful for...   Date

1._____
2._____
3._____
4._____

Today I am grateful for...   Date

1._____
2._____
3._____
4._____

Today I am grateful for...   Date

1._____
2._____
3._____
4._____

Today I am grateful for...   Date

1._____
2._____
3._____
4._____

Today I am grateful for...   Date

1._____
2._____
3._____
4._____

Today I am grateful for...   Date

1._____
2._____
3._____
4._____

My Affirmations for Next Week:

A Garden of Gratitude

> "WE CAN ONLY BE SAID TO BE ALIVE
> IN THOSE MOMENTS WHEN OUR HEARTS
> ARE CONSCIOUS OF OUR TREASURES."
> – THORNTON WILDER

Today I am grateful for...   Date

1._____
2._____
3._____
4._____

Today I am grateful for...   Date

1._____
2._____
3._____
4._____

Today I am grateful for...   Date

1._____
2._____
3._____
4._____

Today I am grateful for...   Date

1._____
2._____
3._____
4._____

Today I am grateful for...   Date

1._____
2._____
3._____
4._____

Today I am grateful for...   Date

1._____
2._____
3._____
4._____

Today I am grateful for...   Date

1._____
2._____
3._____
4._____

My Affirmations for Next Week:

A Garden of Gratitude

> "I LOOKED AROUND AND THOUGHT ABOUT MY LIFE. I FELT GRATEFUL. I NOTICED EVERY DETAIL. THAT IS THE KEY TO TIME TRAVEL. YOU CAN ONLY MOVE IF YOU ARE ACTUALLY IN THE MOMENT. YOU HAVE TO BE WHERE YOU ARE TO GET WHERE YOU NEED TO GO." – AMY POEHLER

Today I am grateful for...   Date

1._____
2._____
3._____
4._____

Today I am grateful for...   Date

1._____
2._____
3._____
4._____

Today I am grateful for...   Date

1._____
2._____
3._____
4._____

Today I am grateful for...   Date

1._____
2._____
3._____
4._____

Today I am grateful for...   Date

1._____
2._____
3._____
4._____

Today I am grateful for...   Date

1._____
2._____
3._____
4._____

Today I am grateful for...   Date

1._____
2._____
3._____
4._____

My Affirmations for Next Week:

A Garden of Gratitude

> "BEING THANKFUL IS NOT ALWAYS EXPERIENCED AS A NATURAL STATE OF EXISTENCE, WE MUST WORK AT IT, AKIN TO A TYPE OF STRENGTH TRAINING FOR THE HEART." – LARISSA GOMEZ

Today I am grateful for...   Date

1._____
2._____
3._____
4._____

Today I am grateful for...   Date

1._____
2._____
3._____
4._____

Today I am grateful for...   Date

1._____
2._____
3._____
4._____

Today I am grateful for...   Date

1._____
2._____
3._____
4._____

Today I am grateful for...   Date

1._____
2._____
3._____
4._____

Today I am grateful for...   Date

1._____
2._____
3._____
4._____

Today I am grateful for...   Date

1._____
2._____
3._____
4._____

My Affirmations for Next Week:

The mind is everything.
What you think –
you become.

– BUDDHA

Affirmations:

Affirmations are one way we can focus our thoughts on the positive things we are and want to be. These affirmations go hand in hand with the practice of gratitude as they both transform our thoughts. Write affirmations about yourself that you want to focus on:

_____

_____

_____

_____

_____

_____

_____

_____

_____

_____

_____

_____

_____

_____

_____

_____

_____

_____

A Garden of Gratitude

> ## "GRATITUDE IS THE SIGN OF NOBLE SOULS."
> ## – AESOP

Today I am grateful for...   Date

1._____
2._____
3._____
4._____

Today I am grateful for...   Date

1._____
2._____
3._____
4._____

Today I am grateful for...   Date

1._____
2._____
3._____
4._____

Today I am grateful for...   Date

1._____
2._____
3._____
4._____

Today I am grateful for...   Date

1._____
2._____
3._____
4._____

Today I am grateful for...   Date

1._____
2._____
3._____
4._____

Today I am grateful for...   Date

1._____
2._____
3._____
4._____

My Affirmations for Next Week:

A Garden of Gratitude

> "HE IS A WISE MAN WHO DOES NOT GRIEVE
> FOR THE THINGS WHICH HE HAS NOT,
> BUT REJOICES FOR THOSE WHICH HE HAS."
> — EPICTETUS

Today I am grateful for...   Date

1._____
2._____
3._____
4._____

Today I am grateful for...   Date

1._____
2._____
3._____
4._____

Today I am grateful for...   Date

1._____
2._____
3._____
4._____

Today I am grateful for...   Date

1._____
2._____
3._____
4._____

Today I am grateful for...   Date

1._____
2._____
3._____
4._____

Today I am grateful for...   Date

1._____
2._____
3._____
4._____

Today I am grateful for...   Date

1._____
2._____
3._____
4._____

My Affirmations for Next Week:

A Garden of Gratitude

> "BE GRATEFUL FOR WHAT YOU ALREADY HAVE WHILE YOU PURSUE YOUR GOALS. IF YOU AREN'T GRATEFUL FOR WHAT YOU ALREADY HAVE, WHAT MAKES YOU THINK YOU WOULD BE HAPPY WITH MORE." – ROY T. BENNETT

Today I am grateful for...   Date

1._____
2._____
3._____
4._____

Today I am grateful for...   Date

1._____
2._____
3._____
4._____

Today I am grateful for...   Date

1._____
2._____
3._____
4._____

Today I am grateful for...   Date

1._____
2._____
3._____
4._____

Today I am grateful for...   Date

1._____
2._____
3._____
4._____

Today I am grateful for...   Date

1._____
2._____
3._____
4._____

Today I am grateful for...   Date

1._____
2._____
3._____
4._____

My Affirmations for Next Week:

A Garden of Gratitude

> "WHEN YOU ARE GRATEFUL,
> FEAR DISAPPEARS AND ABUNDANCE APPEARS."
> – TONY ROBBINS

Today I am grateful for...   Date

1._____
2._____
3._____
4._____

Today I am grateful for...   Date

1._____
2._____
3._____
4._____

Today I am grateful for...   Date

1._____
2._____
3._____
4._____

Today I am grateful for...   Date

1._____
2._____
3._____
4._____

Today I am grateful for...   Date

1._____
2._____
3._____
4._____

Today I am grateful for...   Date

1._____
2._____
3._____
4._____

Today I am grateful for...   Date

1._____
2._____
3._____
4._____

My Affirmations for Next Week:

A Garden of Gratitude

> "IT'S A FUNNY THING ABOUT LIFE, ONCE YOU BEGIN TO TAKE NOTE OF THE THINGS YOU ARE GRATEFUL FOR, YOU BEGIN TO LOSE SIGHT OF THE THINGS THAT YOU LACK." – GERMANY KENT

Today I am grateful for...   Date

1._____
2._____
3._____
4._____

Today I am grateful for...   Date

1._____
2._____
3._____
4._____

Today I am grateful for...   Date

1._____
2._____
3._____
4._____

Today I am grateful for...   Date

1._____
2._____
3._____
4._____

Today I am grateful for...   Date

1._____
2._____
3._____
4._____

Today I am grateful for...   Date

1._____
2._____
3._____
4._____

Today I am grateful for...   Date

1._____
2._____
3._____
4._____

My Affirmations for Next Week:

Gratitude
CREATES
Abundance

A Grateful Heart:

You've been practicing your daily gratitudes for awhile. Now it's time to write the ultimate list of all the things, people, experiences and more that you are grateful for:

A Garden of Gratitude

> "WHEN IT COMES TO LIFE, THE CRITICAL THING IS WHETHER YOU TAKE THINGS FOR GRANTED OR TAKE THEM WITH GRATITUDE." — G.K. CHESTERTON

Today I am grateful for...   Date

1._____
2._____
3._____
4._____

Today I am grateful for...   Date

1._____
2._____
3._____
4._____

Today I am grateful for...   Date

1._____
2._____
3._____
4._____

Today I am grateful for...   Date

1._____
2._____
3._____
4._____

Today I am grateful for...   Date

1._____
2._____
3._____
4._____

Today I am grateful for...   Date

1._____
2._____
3._____
4._____

Today I am grateful for...   Date

1._____
2._____
3._____
4._____

My Affirmations for Next Week:

A Garden of Gratitude

"ENOUGH IS A FEAST."
– BUDDHIST PROVERB

Today I am grateful for...   Date

1._____
2._____
3._____
4._____

Today I am grateful for...   Date

1._____
2._____
3._____
4._____

Today I am grateful for...   Date

1._____
2._____
3._____
4._____

Today I am grateful for...   Date

1._____
2._____
3._____
4._____

Today I am grateful for...   Date

1._____
2._____
3._____
4._____

Today I am grateful for...   Date

1._____
2._____
3._____
4._____

Today I am grateful for...   Date

1._____
2._____
3._____
4._____

My Affirmations for Next Week:

A Garden of Gratitude

> "THE HEART THAT GIVES THANKS IS A HAPPY ONE, FOR WE CANNOT FEEL THANKFUL AND UNHAPPY AT THE SAME TIME." – DOUGLAS WOOD

Today I am grateful for...   Date

1._____
2._____
3._____
4._____

Today I am grateful for...   Date

1._____
2._____
3._____
4._____

Today I am grateful for...   Date

1._____
2._____
3._____
4._____

Today I am grateful for...   Date

1._____
2._____
3._____
4._____

Today I am grateful for...   Date

1._____
2._____
3._____
4._____

Today I am grateful for...   Date

1._____
2._____
3._____
4._____

Today I am grateful for...   Date

1._____
2._____
3._____
4._____

My Affirmations for Next Week:

A Garden of Gratitude

> "DO NOT SPOIL WHAT YOU HAVE BY DESIRING WHAT YOU HAVE NOT; REMEMBER THAT WHAT YOU NOW HAVE WAS ONCE AMONG THE THINGS YOU ONLY HOPED FOR." – EPICURUS

Today I am grateful for...   Date

1._____
2._____
3._____
4._____

Today I am grateful for...   Date

1._____
2._____
3._____
4._____

Today I am grateful for...   Date

1._____
2._____
3._____
4._____

Today I am grateful for...   Date

1._____
2._____
3._____
4._____

Today I am grateful for...   Date

1._____
2._____
3._____
4._____

Today I am grateful for...   Date

1._____
2._____
3._____
4._____

Today I am grateful for...   Date

1._____
2._____
3._____
4._____

My Affirmations for Next Week:

A Garden of Gratitude

> "IF THE ONLY PRAYER YOU SAID WAS THANK YOU,
> THAT WOULD BE ENOUGH."
> – MEISTER ECKHART

Today I am grateful for...   Date

1._____
2._____
3._____
4._____

Today I am grateful for...   Date

1._____
2._____
3._____
4._____

Today I am grateful for...   Date

1._____
2._____
3._____
4._____

Today I am grateful for...   Date

1._____
2._____
3._____
4._____

Today I am grateful for...   Date

1._____
2._____
3._____
4._____

Today I am grateful for...   Date

1._____
2._____
3._____
4._____

Today I am grateful for...   Date

1._____
2._____
3._____
4._____

My Affirmations for Next Week:

"Appreciation is a wonderful thing: It makes what is excellent in others belong to us as well."

- VOLTAIRE

Positive People:

Who are the people in your life that you are most grateful for? What is your relationship with them and how have they impacted your life for the better?

_____

_____

_____

_____

_____

_____

_____

_____

_____

_____

_____

_____

_____

_____

_____

_____

_____

_____

A Garden of Gratitude

> "GRATITUDE IS THE ABILITY
> TO EXPERIENCE LIFE AS A GIFT.
> IT LIBERATES US FROM THE PRISON OF SELF-
> PREOCCUPATION." – JOHN ORTBERG

Today I am grateful for...   Date

1._____
2._____
3._____
4._____

Today I am grateful for...   Date

1._____
2._____
3._____
4._____

Today I am grateful for...   Date

1._____
2._____
3._____
4._____

Today I am grateful for...   Date

1._____
2._____
3._____
4._____

Today I am grateful for...   Date

1._____
2._____
3._____
4._____

Today I am grateful for...   Date

1._____
2._____
3._____
4._____

Today I am grateful for...   Date

1._____
2._____
3._____
4._____

My Affirmations for Next Week:

A Garden of Gratitude

> "REFLECT UPON YOUR PRESENT BLESSINGS,
> OF WHICH EVERY MAN HAS PLENTY;
> NOT ON YOUR PAST MISFORTUNES, OF WHICH ALL MEN
> HAVE SOME." – CHARLES DICKENS

Today I am grateful for...   Date

1._____
2._____
3._____
4._____

Today I am grateful for...   Date

1._____
2._____
3._____
4._____

Today I am grateful for...   Date

1._____
2._____
3._____
4._____

Today I am grateful for...   Date

1._____
2._____
3._____
4._____

Today I am grateful for...   Date

1._____
2._____
3._____
4._____

Today I am grateful for...   Date

1._____
2._____
3._____
4._____

Today I am grateful for...   Date

1._____
2._____
3._____
4._____

My Affirmations for Next Week:

A Garden of Gratitude

> "O LORD THAT LENDS ME LIFE,
> LEND ME A HEART
> REPLETE WITH THANKFULNESS."
> – WILLIAM SHAKESPEARE

Today I am grateful for...   Date

1._____
2._____
3._____
4._____

Today I am grateful for...   Date

1._____
2._____
3._____
4._____

Today I am grateful for...   Date

1._____
2._____
3._____
4._____

Today I am grateful for...   Date

1._____
2._____
3._____
4._____

Today I am grateful for...   Date

1._____
2._____
3._____
4._____

Today I am grateful for...   Date

1._____
2._____
3._____
4._____

Today I am grateful for...   Date

1._____
2._____
3._____
4._____

My Affirmations for Next Week:

A Garden of Gratitude

> ## "THANKFULNESS IS THE QUICKEST PATH TO JOY."
> ## – JEFFERSON BETHKE

Today I am grateful for...   Date

1._____
2._____
3._____
4._____

Today I am grateful for...   Date

1._____
2._____
3._____
4._____

Today I am grateful for...   Date

1._____
2._____
3._____
4._____

Today I am grateful for...   Date

1._____
2._____
3._____
4._____

Today I am grateful for...   Date

1._____
2._____
3._____
4._____

Today I am grateful for...   Date

1._____
2._____
3._____
4._____

Today I am grateful for...   Date

1._____
2._____
3._____
4._____

My Affirmations for Next Week:

A Garden of Gratitude

> "GRATITUDE GOES BEYOND THE 'MINE' AND 'THINE'
> AND CLAIMS THE TRUTH THAT
> ALL OF LIFE IS A PURE GIFT."
> – HENRI J.M. NOUWEN

Today I am grateful for...   Date

1._____
2._____
3._____
4._____

Today I am grateful for...   Date

1._____
2._____
3._____
4._____

Today I am grateful for...   Date

1._____
2._____
3._____
4._____

Today I am grateful for...   Date

1._____
2._____
3._____
4._____

Today I am grateful for...   Date

1._____
2._____
3._____
4._____

Today I am grateful for...   Date

1._____
2._____
3._____
4._____

Today I am grateful for...   Date

1._____
2._____
3._____
4._____

My Affirmations for Next Week:

"Just one small positive thought in the morning can change your whole day."

— DALAI LAMA

Morning Gratitude:

Expressing gratitude in the morning can transform our entire day. What is your morning routine and how can you incorporate the practice of gratitude into it?

_____

_____

_____

_____

_____

_____

_____

_____

_____

_____

_____

_____

_____

_____

_____

_____

_____

_____

_____

_____

A Garden of Gratitude

> "APPRECIATION CAN MAKE A DAY,
> EVEN CHANGE A LIFE. YOUR WILLINGNESS TO PUT IT
> INTO WORDS IS ALL THAT IS NECESSARY."
> – MARGARET COUSINS

Today I am grateful for...   Date

1._____
2._____
3._____
4._____

Today I am grateful for...   Date

1._____
2._____
3._____
4._____

Today I am grateful for...   Date

1._____
2._____
3._____
4._____

Today I am grateful for...   Date

1._____
2._____
3._____
4._____

Today I am grateful for...   Date

1._____
2._____
3._____
4._____

Today I am grateful for...   Date

1._____
2._____
3._____
4._____

Today I am grateful for...   Date

1._____
2._____
3._____
4._____

My Affirmations for Next Week:

A Garden of Gratitude

"GIVE YOURSELF A GIFT OF FIVE MINUTES OF CONTEMPLATION IN AWE OF EVERYTHING YOU SEE. GO OUTSIDE AND TURN YOUR ATTENTION TO THE MANY MIRACLES AROUND YOU. THIS FIVE-MINUTE-A-DAY REGIMEN OF APPRECIATION AND GRATITUDE WILL HELP YOU TO FOCUS YOUR LIFE IN AWE." – WAYNE DYER

Today I am grateful for...　　　Date

1.＿＿＿＿＿＿＿＿＿＿＿＿＿＿＿＿＿
2.＿＿＿＿＿＿＿＿＿＿＿＿＿＿＿＿＿
3.＿＿＿＿＿＿＿＿＿＿＿＿＿＿＿＿＿
4.＿＿＿＿＿＿＿＿＿＿＿＿＿＿＿＿＿

Today I am grateful for...　　　Date

1.＿＿＿＿＿＿＿＿＿＿＿＿＿＿＿＿＿
2.＿＿＿＿＿＿＿＿＿＿＿＿＿＿＿＿＿
3.＿＿＿＿＿＿＿＿＿＿＿＿＿＿＿＿＿
4.＿＿＿＿＿＿＿＿＿＿＿＿＿＿＿＿＿

Today I am grateful for...　　　Date

1.＿＿＿＿＿＿＿＿＿＿＿＿＿＿＿＿＿
2.＿＿＿＿＿＿＿＿＿＿＿＿＿＿＿＿＿
3.＿＿＿＿＿＿＿＿＿＿＿＿＿＿＿＿＿
4.＿＿＿＿＿＿＿＿＿＿＿＿＿＿＿＿＿

Today I am grateful for...   Date

1._____
2._____
3._____
4._____

Today I am grateful for...   Date

1._____
2._____
3._____
4._____

Today I am grateful for...   Date

1._____
2._____
3._____
4._____

Today I am grateful for...   Date

1._____
2._____
3._____
4._____

My Affirmations for Next Week:

A Garden of Gratitude

> "GRATITUDE IS THE HEALTHIEST OF ALL HUMAN EMOTIONS. THE MORE YOU EXPRESS GRATITUDE FOR WHAT YOU HAVE, THE MORE LIKELY YOU WILL HAVE EVEN MORE TO EXPRESS GRATITUDE FOR." – ZIG ZIGLAR

Today I am grateful for...   Date

1._____
2._____
3._____
4._____

Today I am grateful for...   Date

1._____
2._____
3._____
4._____

Today I am grateful for...   Date

1._____
2._____
3._____
4._____

Today I am grateful for...   Date

1._____
2._____
3._____
4._____

Today I am grateful for...   Date

1._____
2._____
3._____
4._____

Today I am grateful for...   Date

1._____
2._____
3._____
4._____

Today I am grateful for...   Date

1._____
2._____
3._____
4._____

My Affirmations for Next Week:

A Garden of Gratitude

> "WHEN A PERSON DOESN'T HAVE GRATITUDE,
> SOMETHING IS MISSING IN HIS OR HER HUMANITY."
> – ELIE WEISEL

Today I am grateful for...   Date

1._____
2._____
3._____
4._____

Today I am grateful for...   Date

1._____
2._____
3._____
4._____

Today I am grateful for...   Date

1._____
2._____
3._____
4._____

Today I am grateful for...   Date

1._____
2._____
3._____
4._____

Today I am grateful for...   Date

1._____
2._____
3._____
4._____

Today I am grateful for...   Date

1._____
2._____
3._____
4._____

Today I am grateful for...   Date

1._____
2._____
3._____
4._____

My Affirmations for Next Week:

A Garden of Gratitude

> "HAPPINESS CANNOT BE TRAVELED TO, OWNED, EARNED, WORN OR CONSUMED. HAPPINESS IS THE SPIRITUAL EXPERIENCE OF LIVING EVERY MINUTE WITH LOVE, GRACE, AND GRATITUDE." - DENIS WAITLEY

Today I am grateful for...   Date

1._____
2._____
3._____
4._____

Today I am grateful for...   Date

1._____
2._____
3._____
4._____

Today I am grateful for...   Date

1._____
2._____
3._____
4._____

Today I am grateful for...   Date

1._____
2._____
3._____
4._____

Today I am grateful for...   Date

1._____
2._____
3._____
4._____

Today I am grateful for...   Date

1._____
2._____
3._____
4._____

Today I am grateful for...   Date

1._____
2._____
3._____
4._____

My Affirmations for Next Week:

"A sense of blessedness
comes from a
change of heart,
not from more blessings."

— MASON COOLEY

Experiences:

What are some life experiences that you are grateful for? This can include trips, education, events, or other moments in life that have shaped you as a person:

A Garden of Gratitude

> ## "GRATITUDE IS RICHES.
> ## COMPLAINT IS POVERTY."
> ## – DORIS DAY

Today I am grateful for...   Date

1._____
2._____
3._____
4._____

Today I am grateful for...   Date

1._____
2._____
3._____
4._____

Today I am grateful for...   Date

1._____
2._____
3._____
4._____

Today I am grateful for...   Date

1._____
2._____
3._____
4._____

Today I am grateful for...   Date

1._____
2._____
3._____
4._____

Today I am grateful for...   Date

1._____
2._____
3._____
4._____

Today I am grateful for...   Date

1._____
2._____
3._____
4._____

My Affirmations for Next Week:

A Garden of Gratitude

> "IF YOU WANT TO TURN YOUR LIFE AROUND,
> TRY THANKFULNESS.
> IT WILL CHANGE YOUR LIFE MIGHTILY."
> – GERALD GOOD

Today I am grateful for...   Date

1._____
2._____
3._____
4._____

Today I am grateful for...   Date

1._____
2._____
3._____
4._____

Today I am grateful for...   Date

1._____
2._____
3._____
4._____

Today I am grateful for...   Date

1._____
2._____
3._____
4._____

Today I am grateful for...   Date

1._____
2._____
3._____
4._____

Today I am grateful for...   Date

1._____
2._____
3._____
4._____

Today I am grateful for...   Date

1._____
2._____
3._____
4._____

My Affirmations for Next Week:

A Garden of Gratitude

"THIS A WONDERFUL DAY. I'VE NEVER SEEN THIS ONE BEFORE." – MAYA ANGELOU

Today I am grateful for...   Date

1._____
2._____
3._____
4._____

Today I am grateful for...   Date

1._____
2._____
3._____
4._____

Today I am grateful for...   Date

1._____
2._____
3._____
4._____

Today I am grateful for...   Date

1._____
2._____
3._____
4._____

Today I am grateful for...   Date

1._____
2._____
3._____
4._____

Today I am grateful for...   Date

1._____
2._____
3._____
4._____

Today I am grateful for...   Date

1._____
2._____
3._____
4._____

My Affirmations for Next Week:

A Garden of Gratitude

> "IN LIFE, ONE HAS A CHOICE TO TAKE ONE OF TWO
> PATHS: TO WAIT FOR SOME SPECIAL DAY—
> OR TO CELEBRATE EACH SPECIAL DAY."
> – RASHEED OGUNLARU

Today I am grateful for...   Date

1. _____
2. _____
3. _____
4. _____

Today I am grateful for...   Date

1. _____
2. _____
3. _____
4. _____

Today I am grateful for...   Date

1. _____
2. _____
3. _____
4. _____

Today I am grateful for...   Date

1._____
2._____
3._____
4._____

Today I am grateful for...   Date

1._____
2._____
3._____
4._____

Today I am grateful for...   Date

1._____
2._____
3._____
4._____

Today I am grateful for...   Date

1._____
2._____
3._____
4._____

My Affirmations for Next Week:

A Garden of Gratitude

> "GRATITUDE ALSO OPENS YOUR EYES TO THE LIMITLESS POTENTIAL OF THE UNIVERSE, WHILE DISSATISFACTION CLOSES YOUR EYES TO IT."
> – STEPHEN RICHARDS

Today I am grateful for...   Date

1._____
2._____
3._____
4._____

Today I am grateful for...   Date

1._____
2._____
3._____
4._____

Today I am grateful for...   Date

1._____
2._____
3._____
4._____

Today I am grateful for...   Date

1._____
2._____
3._____
4._____

Today I am grateful for...   Date

1._____
2._____
3._____
4._____

Today I am grateful for...   Date

1._____
2._____
3._____
4._____

Today I am grateful for...   Date

1._____
2._____
3._____
4._____

My Affirmations for Next Week:

How lucky I am
to have something
that makes
saying goodbye
so hard.

– A.A. MILNE

Life Lessons:

Some life lessons are learned from successes, while others are learned from failure. Share some life lessons that you are grateful for and what you learned:

_____
_____
_____
_____
_____
_____
_____
_____
_____
_____
_____
_____
_____
_____
_____
_____
_____
_____
_____
_____
_____

A Garden of Gratitude

> "THE STRUGGLE ENDS
> WHERE GRATITUDE BEGINS."
> – NEALE DONALD WALSH

Today I am grateful for...   Date

1._____
2._____
3._____
4._____

Today I am grateful for...   Date

1._____
2._____
3._____
4._____

Today I am grateful for...   Date

1._____
2._____
3._____
4._____

Today I am grateful for...   Date

1._____
2._____
3._____
4._____

Today I am grateful for...   Date

1._____
2._____
3._____
4._____

Today I am grateful for...   Date

1._____
2._____
3._____
4._____

Today I am grateful for...   Date

1._____
2._____
3._____
4._____

My Affirmations for Next Week:

A Garden of Gratitude

> "THE MORE YOU USE GRATITUDE EVERY DAY,
> THE GREATER THE GOOD
> YOU WILL BRING INTO YOUR LIFE."
> – RHONDA BYRNE

Today I am grateful for...   Date

1._____
2._____
3._____
4._____

Today I am grateful for...   Date

1._____
2._____
3._____
4._____

Today I am grateful for...   Date

1._____
2._____
3._____
4._____

Today I am grateful for...   Date

1._____
2._____
3._____
4._____

Today I am grateful for...   Date

1._____
2._____
3._____
4._____

Today I am grateful for...   Date

1._____
2._____
3._____
4._____

Today I am grateful for...   Date

1._____
2._____
3._____
4._____

My Affirmations for Next Week:

A Garden of Gratitude

> "GRATITUDE OPENS THE DOOR TO THE POWER, THE WISDOM, THE CREATIVITY OF THE UNIVERSE."
> – DEEPAK CHOPRA

Today I am grateful for...   Date

1._____
2._____
3._____
4._____

Today I am grateful for...   Date

1._____
2._____
3._____
4._____

Today I am grateful for...   Date

1._____
2._____
3._____
4._____

Today I am grateful for...   Date

1._____
2._____
3._____
4._____

Today I am grateful for...   Date

1._____
2._____
3._____
4._____

Today I am grateful for...   Date

1._____
2._____
3._____
4._____

Today I am grateful for...   Date

1._____
2._____
3._____
4._____

My Affirmations for Next Week:

A Garden of Gratitude

> "THERE IS A CALMNESS
> TO A LIFE LIVED IN GRATITUDE,
> A QUIET JOY."
> – RALPH H. BLUM

Today I am grateful for...   Date

1._____
2._____
3._____
4._____

Today I am grateful for...   Date

1._____
2._____
3._____
4._____

Today I am grateful for...   Date

1._____
2._____
3._____
4._____

Today I am grateful for...   Date

1._____
2._____
3._____
4._____

Today I am grateful for...   Date

1._____
2._____
3._____
4._____

Today I am grateful for...   Date

1._____
2._____
3._____
4._____

Today I am grateful for...   Date

1._____
2._____
3._____
4._____

My Affirmations for Next Week:

A Garden of Gratitude

> "GRATITUDE IS THE SINGLE MOST
> IMPORTANT INGREDIENT TO LIVING
> A SUCCESSFUL AND FULFILLING LIFE."
> – JACK CANFIELD

Today I am grateful for...   Date

1._____
2._____
3._____
4._____

Today I am grateful for...   Date

1._____
2._____
3._____
4._____

Today I am grateful for...   Date

1._____
2._____
3._____
4._____

Today I am grateful for...   Date

1._____
2._____
3._____
4._____

Today I am grateful for...   Date

1._____
2._____
3._____
4._____

Today I am grateful for...   Date

1._____
2._____
3._____
4._____

Today I am grateful for...   Date

1._____
2._____
3._____
4._____

My Affirmations for Next Week:

GRATITUDE
turns what we have
INTO ENOUGH.

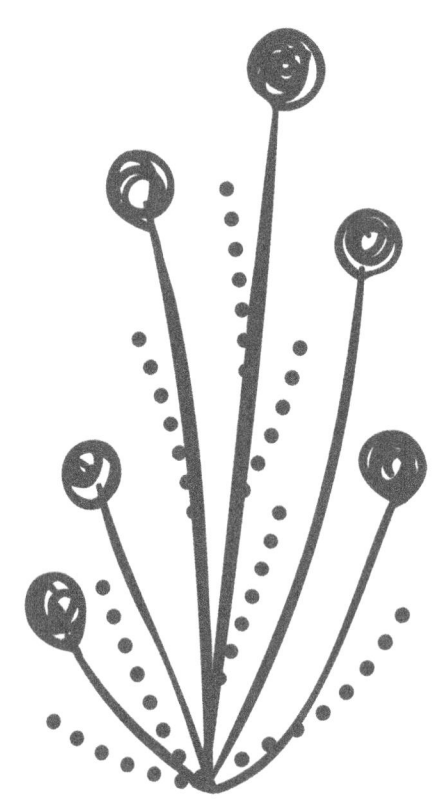

Life's Comforts:

Things can often bring us joy, bring back beautiful memories and offer comfort. What are the physical things in your life that you are grateful for?

_____

_____

_____

_____

_____

_____

_____

_____

_____

_____

_____

_____

_____

_____

_____

_____

_____

_____

A Garden of Gratitude

"THE REAL GIFT OF GRATITUDE
IS THAT THE MORE GRATEFUL YOU ARE,
THE MORE PRESENT YOU BECOME."
– ROBERT HOLDEN

Today I am grateful for...   Date

1._____
2._____
3._____
4._____

Today I am grateful for...   Date

1._____
2._____
3._____
4._____

Today I am grateful for...   Date

1._____
2._____
3._____
4._____

Today I am grateful for...   Date

1._____
2._____
3._____
4._____

Today I am grateful for...   Date

1._____
2._____
3._____
4._____

Today I am grateful for...   Date

1._____
2._____
3._____
4._____

Today I am grateful for...   Date

1._____
2._____
3._____
4._____

My Affirmations for Next Week:

A Garden of Gratitude

> "GRATITUDE IS THE FAIREST BLOSSOM
> WHICH SPRINGS FROM THE SOUL."
> – HENRY WARD BEECHER.

Today I am grateful for...   Date

1._____
2._____
3._____
4._____

Today I am grateful for...   Date

1._____
2._____
3._____
4._____

Today I am grateful for...   Date

1._____
2._____
3._____
4._____

Today I am grateful for...   Date

1._____
2._____
3._____
4._____

Today I am grateful for...   Date

1._____
2._____
3._____
4._____

Today I am grateful for...   Date

1._____
2._____
3._____
4._____

Today I am grateful for...   Date

1._____
2._____
3._____
4._____

My Affirmations for Next Week:

DO YOU LIKE FREEBIES?

EMAIL US AT:

GVPUBLISHINGCO@GMAIL.COM

USE SUBJECT: GARDEN

AND WE'LL SEND YOU SOME!

Thank you for your purchase.
We are so grateful for you.

Made in the USA
Monee, IL
08 December 2020

51489126R00075